NOURISHING WISDOM *for* LIFE

A Chinese Guide to Health for Families & New Mothers

SYLVIA L. QUAN

Dedication

This book is dedicated to my daughters, Caroline, Kristen, and Katherine, my existing grandchildren, and any others I may be blessed with in the future. My hope is that both my family and yours will benefit from the traditional Chinese household wisdom contained herein, both in general and specifically with regard to postpartum care for women. As with most traditional care, much of its emphasis is on food, and so this has taken the loose form of a recipe book. Much of this ancient knowledge has come to me through my own family, and this book comes from my desire to keep passing it on through the next generations.

Published in 2019

Text and diagrams copyright © 2019 Sylvia L. Quan

All rights reserved. No portion of this book may be reproduced, stored in a retrieval system, or transmitted in any form or by any means, mechanical, electronic, photocopying, recording, or otherwise, without written permission from the author.

ISBN: 978-1-0931-4354-6

Editor: Rachel M. Coleman
Designer: Katherine Quan Ahmann
DesignQStudio.com

Disclaimer:

This book provides anecdotal information—passed down through generations—on the traditional Chinese approach to postpartum care and other related issues (specifically, from the Guangdong region). Its goal, as should be the case with any postpartum care, is to replenish, restore, and strengthen a woman and her health after childbirth. My approach to this is based on thousands of years of tradition and culture but is not meant to be a replacement for a certified physician. Please consult with your physician on your own particular health needs. In particular, the tonic recipes are not designed to replace any medication prescribed by your doctor and as with all medicine, traditional or otherwise, no one can make any guarantees. The authors and publisher disclaim all liability in connection with the use of this book.

www.NourishingWisdom.net

Table of Contents

My Story 1

PART 1

The Three Theories of Traditional Chinese Medicine 7

- The Theory of *Yin* and *Yang* 8
  - The Opposition of *Yin* and *Yang* 10
  - The *Yin* and *Yang* Properties of Food 11
- The Concept of the Twelve Meridians 12
  - *Zang* and *Fu* Organs 13
  - Meridians and Orifices 14
- The Law of the Five Elements 16
  - Emotions and the Five Elements 18
  - The Five Flavors of Food 19

PART 2

The Essential Month 22

Recipes
- Phase I: Purging, Cleansing, and Strengthening 25
- Phase II: Nourishing 35
- Phase III: Restoring 38

PART 3

TCM Tips for the Family 42

Stories 44

MY STORY

I HAVE BEEN EXPOSED MY ENTIRE LIFE, IN ONE WAY OR ANOTHER, TO THE CHINESE APPROACH TO POSTPARTUM CARE AND OTHER RELATED ISSUES. It started with learning from my own mother and aunts and expanded by learning from those with more expertise than me. Along the way, I have helped many women, my own friends and daughters included, recover from childbirth and issues related to it. I write from what I know: a Chinese approach, handed down from previous generations, combined with some Yong Shu Yang (YSY) Therapy, which attempts to integrate the technical approach of western medicine with the more holistic approach of eastern medicine. In order to explain why I am writing this book, I must tell a little of my story—how I came to this knowledge, and why I wish to pass it on.

Early life

China is a vast country made up of many different ethnicities and cultures. The recipes in this book are based on the traditional wisdom of the region in which I grew up, Guangdong, a southern province.

I am my mother's tenth child of five boys and five girls. Shortly after I was born, our whole family moved back to China from the Seychelles soon after the Communist takeover. We moved to Shunde, our ancestral land in Guangdong Province, where my paternal grandparents lived. Since Hong Kong was a British colony and migration was restricted by the Chinese government, my father and older siblings had to be smuggled into Hong Kong. My mother felt I was too young to take the risky voyage, so she and I stayed behind in the village. I was surrounded by natural beauty there: our house was by the river, from which we would eat fish, and we had a beautiful garden and many fruit trees, from which our family would also eat. However, this somewhat idyllic life did not last. In order to be united with the rest of the family, my mother and I moved to Canton (subsequently renamed Guangzhou) and were smuggled from there to Hong Kong a few years later. But even in Hong Kong—away from the beauty of our place in Shunde—my mother provided a stable and cozy atmosphere.

Growing up, I was often enveloped by aromas from the kitchen of herbal soups which had been concocted by my mother and my aunties. These soups were not simply made to taste good (though they did!): some were for the girls to help with the time before and after menses, some were for strengthening the boys' vitality, some were for balancing the body when it was either on the "cooling" or "warming" side, the list goes on. But there were always soups and other delicious dishes mixed with certain kinds of meat or dried seafood, vegetables, and herbs for every symptom we had. Mother would explain to us the properties or nature of the ingredients along with when they should be used. With this knowledge, she would treat the condition of each of her children's ever-changing health, whether that change was due to the evolving nature of our bodies or just the changing of the seasons.

Our house in Hong Kong was always busy. Not only did my siblings and I live with my parents, but our household also included seven members of our extended family. We lived in a spacious three-story building in Kowloon, so fortunately we were not cramped, but the house was always bustling with activity. Mother was in charge of planning daily meals for the 20-plus-person household; the younger women and two domestic helpers handled the cooking under Mother's supervision. As the youngest, I had the privilege of accompanying my mother to the market daily (and often times, twice daily) after school. Thus, through first-hand experience, I was able to observe how to select the best piece of meat, the best quality vegetables, and

Lau family photo. I am in the front row, next to my mother. Hong Kong, circa 1954.

My Story

the proper color of herbs. There is simply no better way to understand food than to be, literally, hands on, and I had that experience in spades with my mother. Soon I began to see the food in the market with my mother's eyes. I could discriminate good from bad, fresh from stale, flavorful from insipid.

After my siblings married, my mother's (and by extension, my) busiest time was always after the birth of one of her grandchildren. According to Chinese tradition, a new mother should consume many and varied specially-prepared herbal tonics, soups, and other dishes in order to restore her health. Additionally, a new mother is expected to stay indoors for one month after the birth of her child. My mother took on the responsibility of taking care of her daughters and daughters-in-law during this postpartum period, which consists of thirty days of rest. She knew how important "*boh*"—a Cantonese word that means replenishing, nourishing, and restoring—was for the new mother. Again, because of my position as the youngest child of a very large family, I was fortunate enough to witness the postpartum care for over 20 births. My education into Chinese medicine was thus first and foremost experiential; I learned through helping my mother, being with her and my aunties while they cared for new mothers, and simply living the life into which I had been born.

My mother and I, circa 1959

YSY Therapy

My education into health and medicine, however, did not stop with what I learned from my mother. Eventually, I emigrated to the United States from Hong Kong—Houston, Texas, to be specific—and it was here that I encountered YSY Therapy. Named after the inventor, Dr. Yong Shu Yang, YSY Therapy was later recognized as YSY Medicine by the Chinese Academy of Sciences in the 1990s. Dr. Yang attempts to combine the technical precision of western medicine with the ancient knowledge and more holistic approach of Chinese medicine. She graduated from China's Fourth Military Medical University in 1965[1] as a trained surgeon, but she also has extensive knowledge of traditional Chinese medicine.

During her first fifteen years of medical practice, Dr. Yang saw that conventional western medical techniques were, simply put, not enough to help many of her patients. She sought alternative and non-invasive medical solutions for patients, leading her to obtain advanced degrees in Chinese Medicine, acupuncture, and massage from Hunan Chinese Medical University. Additionally, Dr. Yang has studied and practiced *Qi Gong* (energy manipulation) her entire life,[2] and saw the need for integrating all of these natural approaches into her research

---

1. www.ysy.com.
2. Ibid.

and practice of medicine. Energy is a key concept and healing tool in traditional Chinese medical practice, and Dr. Yang wished to integrate this understanding with western practices. This integration led to the invention of YSY Therapy. YSY Therapy regulates blood and energy circulation along one's meridians, which are energy pathways in the body, in harmony with the condition of a person's internal organs and the external environment. In addition to suggesting lifestyle adjustments and providing psychological advice, YSY practitioners use their bare hands, generating energy with varying intensity, to trigger and unblock meridians, purge toxins, invigorate blood flow, and optimize energy balance. As a result of the clinical success of her integrative approach to medicine, Dr. Yang has become incredibly well known in China for YSY Therapy, which was awarded the Most Significant Scientific Invention by the Chinese Ministry of Health in 1988. In the 1990s, it evolved into a systematic practice of energy medicine and was renamed YSY Medicine. It has been taught in medical schools in China.

I was introduced to Dr. Yang by a mutual friend while she worked as a researcher in Houston. Dr. Yang did not speak English, so I often assisted as her interpreter with her research team. This was the beginning of a long friendship, from which I reaped many benefits. During this time, I was able to observe, question, and learn about her unique field of holistic healing, which is in harmony with traditional Chinese culture.

Blowing out the candles from my 70th birthday cake with my grandchildren.

PART 1

THE THREE THEORIES OF TRADITIONAL CHINESE MEDICINE

IN ORDER TO UNDERSTAND THE EFFECTS OF THE HERBAL RECIPES INCLUDED herein, we need to understand some of the basic concepts, philosophy, and theories of traditional Chinese medicine (TCM). TCM is based on three major theories, but all three theories share one main principle: all living beings have life force or energy that sustains them. This energy is called *qi*, and anything that lives is alive because of this energy.

TCM Theories:

- The Theory of *Yin* and *Yang*
- The Concept of the Twelve Meridians
- The Law of the Five Elements

Traditional Chinese medicine places an emphasis on food therapy, which differs from western medicine's emphasis on treating conditions through drugs. Food plays a vital part in TCM because it helps to balance energy in the body. Food can heal the body, but this in turn means that food can also hurt the body. One must pay attention to what one consumes.

Conventional fields of western nutrition classify food in terms of its chemical composition, including the calories, carbohydrates, proteins, fats, and other nutrients that it contains. Traditional Chinese medicine, on the other hand, categorizes food as 涼 *leung* ("cooling"), 熱氣 *yiht hei* ("heaty"),[1] and neutral. It uses the nature of the foods to balance the body's *yin* and *yang*.

TCM HEALING AND TREATMENT METHODS
- Chinese herbology
- Acupuncture and acupressure
- Exercise (*Tai Chi*, *Qi Gong*, other branches of martial arts, etc.)
- *Tui Na*, also known as Chinese medical massage
- Cupping
- *Gua Sha*, also known as scraping[2]

---

1. Though not a frequently used word, "heaty" in fact was included in the December 2016 update of the *Oxford English Dictionary*. Its definition: "(adjective): Of a disease, food, or medicine: that warms, stimulates, or energizes the body. Also of a person's constitution: sensitive to heat; susceptible to disorders such as fever, sore throat, excessive thirst, etc."
2. See www.healthline.com/health/gua-sha.

THE THEORY OF *YIN* AND *YANG*

To begin, we need to understand the concept of energy and the two types of energy force. Our body is made up of a network of meridians or channels in which blood and *qi*, i.e., energy, are circulated. According to Albert Szent-Gyorgyi, a biochemist and Nobel Prize winner from Hungary, "In every culture and in every medical tradition before ours, healing was accomplished by moving energy."

Qi, 氣 (pronounced "chee"): A one character/word which includes multiple meanings. *Qi* refers to life-force, or the human energy. The word "*qi*" is used to express strength, anger, nervous influx, electricity, etc. *Qi* affects the blood circulation, and this dictates where blood goes and how it flows in the body. When there is insufficient *qi* in a certain part of the body, there will be insufficient blood in that part as well. *Qi* is classified as *yin* or *yang*. *Yin* means negative and *yang* means positive. Both fundamental forces co-exist in the human body and in nature. All matter in the universe results from the interaction of *yin* and *yang*.

Yin qi and *yang qi* are mutually dependent forces that co-exist in nature. They are a dynamic balance of opposite, yet complementary, energies that form a whole. They are inseparable and interpenetrating. The nature of the *qi* that circulates in human bodies transforms from *yin* to *yang* and from *yang* to *yin* without end, constantly developing and changing, but always in equilibrium. It is never *yin* vs. *yang* but, rather, that *yin* and *yang* must always be kept in proper tension in order for us to achieve balance. Illness results from a disorder of *qi* which imbalances the *yin* and the *yang* in our bodies. Health is maintained by an optimal balance of these two energies.

The chart below attempts to illustrate the characteristics of *yin* and *yang*:

ENERGY/NATURE	YIN	YANG
Human	Female	Male
Environment	Dark	Light
	Shade	Sun
	Interior	Exterior
	Cold	Hot
	Water	Fire
	Moist	Dry
	Soft	Hard
	Earth	Sky
Characteristic	Slow	Rapid
	Matter	Energy
Human Behavior	Suppressing	Uplifting
	Inhibition	Excitement
Color of Qi	Dark	Light
Energy	Descending	Ascending
	Contracting	Expanding
	Conserving	Transforming
Temperature	Cold	Warm
Food	Nourishing	Strengthening

In the body, *yin* tends toward cold, while *yang* tends toward heat. In the human body, *qi* promotes blood flow. If *qi* is impeded, blood circulation slows or stops. *Yin* is the energy of maintenance. It governs blood flow and maintains body cells. *Yang* is the energy of growth and reproduction. It promotes cell growth and the function of organs. As we grow older, our *yang* energy diminishes.

In nature, an abundance of *yang* energy emerges when the sun rises. The atmosphere is filled with *yang qi*. The morning is therefore the best time to harness *yang qi* by meditating, practicing *Tai Chi* or *Qi Gong*, or by exercising outdoors. In the late afternoon, as the sun sets, *yang qi* decreases, and *yin qi* rises.

The Opposition of Yin *and* Yang

Under normal conditions, the human body maintains a relative physiological balance through the mutual opposition of *yin* and *yang*. If there is an excess or deficiency of *yin* or *yang* in the body, this relative balance will be disrupted and health issues will arise.

Illness results from the obstruction of the *qi* in the meridians or channels (see next section) due to the seven major causes listed below:

- Genetics: blocked meridians can be genetically inherited. A parent with high blood pressure may have blocked heart and liver meridians, and this can be passed on to his children. His children are at higher risk of having blockages in the heart and liver meridians later in life, and therefore preventative efforts to unblock these meridians should be taken as they may reduce the child's chance of developing high blood pressure or postpone the onset of high blood pressure.

- Birth Defects: some babies are born with structural or metabolic birth defects that cause *qi* obstruction in their meridians. For example, heart defects are often related to *qi* blockage in the heart meridian. Proper nutritional care and natural treatments aimed at invigorating *qi* and blood flow in the baby's heart meridian can help to alleviate symptoms like difficulty breathing or a heart murmur.

- Traumatic Injuries: injuries that result from playing sports or a car accident can damage a person's body and the functions of their internal organs, leading to temporary or permanent *qi* obstruction in the body depending on the severity of the injury. Concussions, a common injury, usually block the liver and gallbladder meridians; clearing these blockages can relieve headaches and reduce memory loss.

- Surgery: surgical incisions interfere with normal *qi* flow in its surrounding meridians, and this may cause malfunction of the linked organs.

- Side effects of medication and drugs: chemical components of drugs and medications can leave residue inside the body, and these unwanted chemicals can cause a buildup of toxins in the meridians, which then creates *qi* obstruction.

- Emotional issues: the regular ups and downs of human emotion can also affect *qi* flow. For example, sadness and grief over the loss of a loved one may cause insomnia, which leads to *qi* stagnation in the heart meridian. If insomnia persists, irritation and poor cognitive performance may result, which are signs of excessive *yang qi* in the body. This is the time to cool down the body to restore *qi* flow within the heart meridian.

- Environment: harsh climate and environmental factors also have an effect on our *yin-yang* balance. A change of season, a strange weather pattern, heavy pollution or even contaminated water can throw our *qi* out of balance and cause *qi* obstruction in the body.

The Yin *and* Yang *Properties of Food*

As we have discussed, *yin* and *yang* energy must always be in balance. If one force dominates, then it creates a deficiency in the other. In a healthy physical state, the *yin* and *yang* work with each other, adjusting back and forth as needed. The two most significant qualities in the healing use of food are their warming or cooling properties.

Yin foods are cool in nature. They moisten the body and have a nourishing effect. **Yang foods** are warm in nature. The *yin* or *yang* characteristics of a certain food have less to do with a food's actual temperature and more to do with how they affect the body and the body's *qi*. Even though a boiling cup of chrysanthemum tea is hot in temperature, it has *yin* properties and therefore will tend to cool down the internal heat of the body.

A body with excess heat (hyper-*yang*) needs cooling foods to bring the body back into balance, just as a body with excess cold (hyper-*yin*) needs warming foods. Some foods are useful for promoting *qi* while others are useful for promoting blood. For example, beef is beneficial for those with *yang* deficiency conditions, but not for those with *yang* excess.

New mothers tend to have hyper-*yin* as a result of giving birth. The traditional soups used by Chinese households during the postpartum rest period serve as remedies to invigorate the *yang qi* but also nourish the *yin*. This promotes a smooth and balanced flowing of the *yin* and *yang qi*. Consequently, vital blood-flow and in turn strength, will be restored.

Common yin *foods include:*

- soy products, such as tofu and soybean sprouts
- fish, scallops, abalone, clams, etc.
- fruit, such as watermelon, grapefruit, star fruit, orange, lemon, blueberry, strawberry, etc.
- vegetables, such as watercress, cucumbers, carrots, bitter melon, mustard greens, spinach, tomato and lettuce

Common yang *foods include:*

- beef, lamb, chicken, turkey, pork, etc.
- warm spices such as ginger, cinnamon, nutmeg, and pepper
- glutinous rice and sesame oil
- alcoholic beverages
- sweet vegetables such as yam, and fruits such as apples and peaches.

Chinese medicine also categorizes foods according to five different flavors, which I will cover more in the subsequent sections. I should note now, however, that these five flavors are themselves classified according to *yin* and *yang*:

- Sour, bitter, and salty flavors are generally *yin* in nature.
- Spicy and sweet flavors are generally *yang* in nature.

THE CONCEPT OF THE TWELVE MERIDIANS

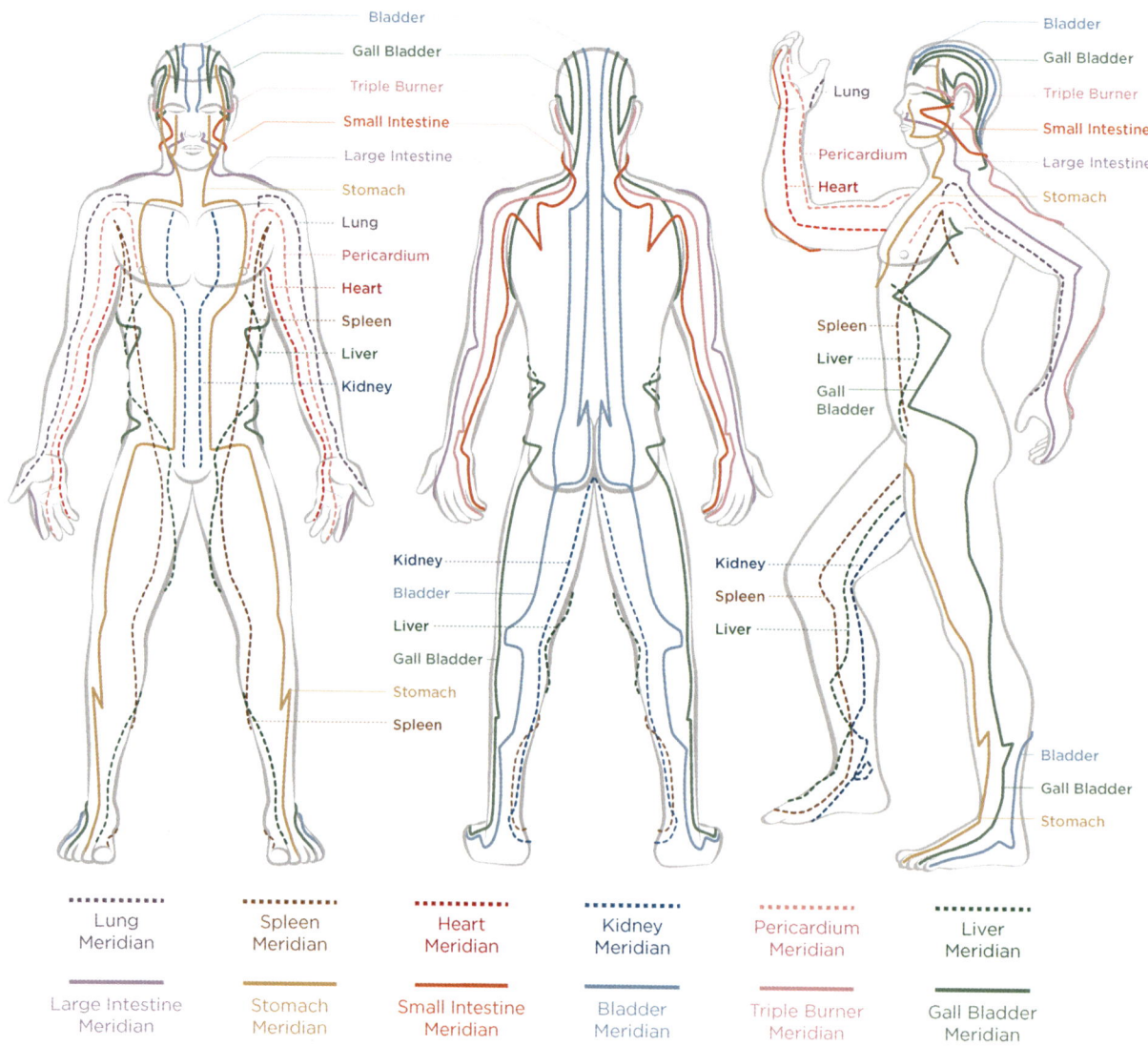

Though I am not an expert, I can provide a basic understanding of the Twelve Meridians (or channels), which is important to understand why TCM functions as it does. Throughout the body, there is a network for the fundamental substances of *qi*, blood, and bodily fluids. This network makes up the meridian system: a vast yet intricate web of delicate, interconnecting lines that links different parts of the body together. Meridian pathways supply vital energy and blood to every part of the body, and keeping these pathways clear of obstruction allows the body to perform as it should. Each of these pathways is made of many acupoints, also known as acupressure or acupuncture points. According to conventional Chinese wisdom, the Meridian System explains how we live and why we become sick. Illness occurs when there is an obstruction of a meridian: *qi* becomes sluggish and stagnant and thus affects the flow of blood and other bodily fluids. The *qi* of a new mother who has just given birth is weak. Proper food and care are needed to revitalize the flow of *qi*.

Each meridian connects with a specific organ, circulates through a certain part of the body to the surface of the skin, and comes into contact with the external environment. Since the Twelve Meridians make up the majority of the meridian system, they are known as the principal channels. The meridian system is not analogous to the circulatory system. Conventional anatomy and physiology would not be able to identify these pathways in a physical sense in the way that blood vessels can be identified.

YIN MERIDIANS	*YANG* MERIDIANS
Lung Meridian	Large Intestine Meridian
Spleen Meridian	Stomach Meridian
Heart Meridian	Small Intestine Meridian
Kidney Meridian	Bladder Meridian
Pericardium Meridian	Triple Burner Meridian
Liver Meridian	Gall Bladder Meridian

Additionally, each primary meridian is categorized as either *yin* or *yang* and matches with a corresponding meridian to create a total of six *yin-yang* pairs. For example, the *yin* Lung Meridian corresponds with the *yang* Large Intestine Meridian. The *yin* meridians flow up the body while the *yang* meridians flow down the body. The Twelve Meridians on the left side of the body are symmetrical to the right side of the body. The meridians vary in depth. Sequentially, the Liver Meridian is the deepest level and the Lung Meridian is closest to the surface.

Zang *and* Fu *Organs*

The twelve meridians are named for their corresponding organs and limb positions: five *yin* organs called *Zang* and six *yang* organs called *Fu*. The five *Zang*, or solid organs are the Lung, Spleen, Heart, Kidney, and Liver. The six *Fu*, or hollow organs are the Large Intestine, Stomach, Small Intestine, Bladder, Triple Burner, and Gall Bladder.

The *Zang-Fu* are not equivalent to the anatomical organs, their names are often capitalized. They are functional entities first, with a correspondence (but not an exact equivalence) to the organs. *Zang-Fu* organs relate to processing functions of the body. The *Zang* organs specialize in manufacturing, collecting, and storing while the *Fu* organs specialize in moving and transforming actions for substances in the body. It is also worth noting that *Zang-Fu* organs and their corresponding meridians should not be thought of as being identical with the anatomical organs of the body. Each *Zang* is paired with a *Fu*, and each pair is assigned to one of the Five Elements. The *Zang-Fu* are also connected to the twelve primary meridians—each *yin* meridian is attached to a *Zang* organ, and each *yang* meridian is attached to a *Fu* organ.

The *yin* Pericardium is paired with the *yang* Triple Burner (*sanjiao*). Both of these are conceptual organs found only in TCM theories. The Triple Burner Meridian does not refer to a discrete anatomical structure: it is a functional energy system that regulates the activities of other organs. It refers to three equally divided portions of the body: upper, middle, and lower. However, the Triple Burner Meridian does not run within these three parts of the body. The Upper Burner refers to the chest area and controls intake. The Middle Burner refers to the abdomen and controls transformation. The Lower Burner refers to the pelvis and controls elimination.

Meridians and Orifices

Each organ meridian opens at one particular orifice of the body and connects with a particular tissue. For example, lungs connect with the nose as an orifice and skin as the tissue. Think of it this way: the orifice is an opening which connects the corresponding meridian to the external environment so that it can receive external *yin* and *yang qi* and release toxins. Practitioners of Chinese medicine observe the conditions of these orifices to gather sufficient information to make in-depth diagnoses. For example, if the bones or teeth (which are associated with the Kidney Meridian) are not strong, the root of the problem is likely a blockage of the Kidney Meridian. Herbs, beef, pork, or chicken bone broth would be prescribed to strengthen the kidneys and improve bone health.

- *Lung Meridian*: opens at the nose/nostrils. It affects or manifests through the skin. If the lungs are healthy, the skin will look radiant. If this meridian is blocked, people will suffer upper respiratory problems, such as allergies, asthma, etc.
- *Spleen Meridian*: opens at the mouth. It affects or manifests in the muscles.
- *Heart Meridian*: opens at the tongue. It affects or manifests in the blood vessels. If people have a cardiovascular condition, this meridian is blocked.
- *Kidney Meridian*: opens at the ears. It affects or manifests in the bone. If people experience ear infections or osteoporosis, TCM practitioners would examine the condition of this meridian.
- *Liver Meridian*: opens at the eyes. It affects or manifests in the tendons and ligaments. If people have glaucoma or tendonitis, this meridian needs to be treated.

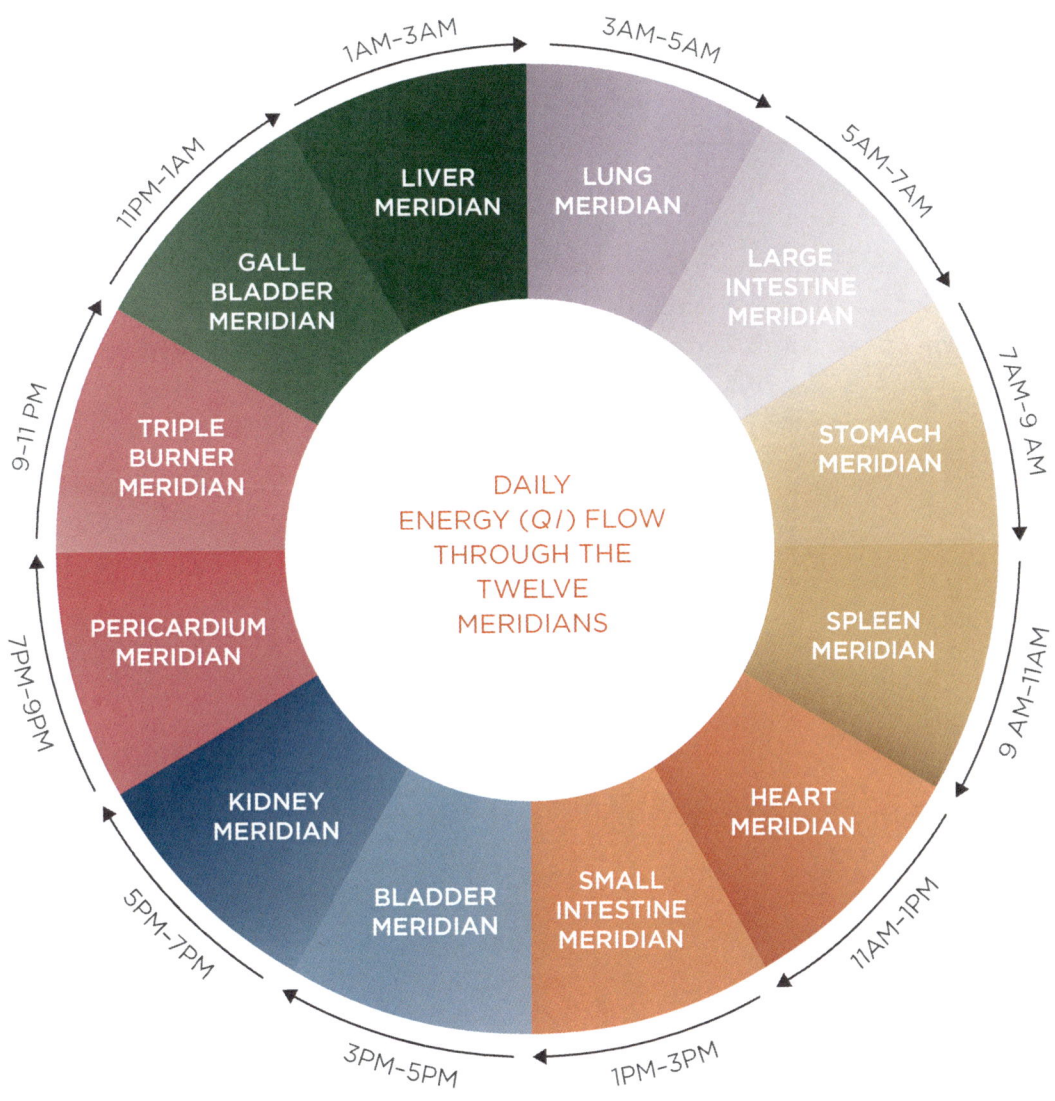

Each meridian is related to one of the Five Elements (discussed in the next section) and is most active at a certain time of the day or night. While *qi* flows continuously throughout the body 24 hours a day, it focuses on a particular organ meridian every two hours while maintaining the functions of the other meridians. The meridians vary in depth. Sequentially, the Liver Meridian is the deepest level and the Lung Meridian is closest to the surface.

THE LAW OF THE FIVE ELEMENTS

The Five Elements refer to the five elements that exist in nature: Metal, Water, Wood, Fire, and Earth. They play an important role in all aspects of Chinese culture, from the way we approach food and medicine to the way we live. It is universally accepted, not just in Chinese culture, that the Five Elements are all interconnected, interdependent upon each other. Very similarly, the meridians of the body are also interrelated. Just as an overabundance of one element will inevitably affect the other elements in nature, an imbalance in one meridian will have a residual effect throughout the rest of the human body. To take it a step further, the Five Elements can also explain how external factors, such as the environment, food, and herbs can influence organs, their corresponding meridians, and the functioning of the body. They also provide an understanding and representation of the dynamic balance of opposites and the processes of change.

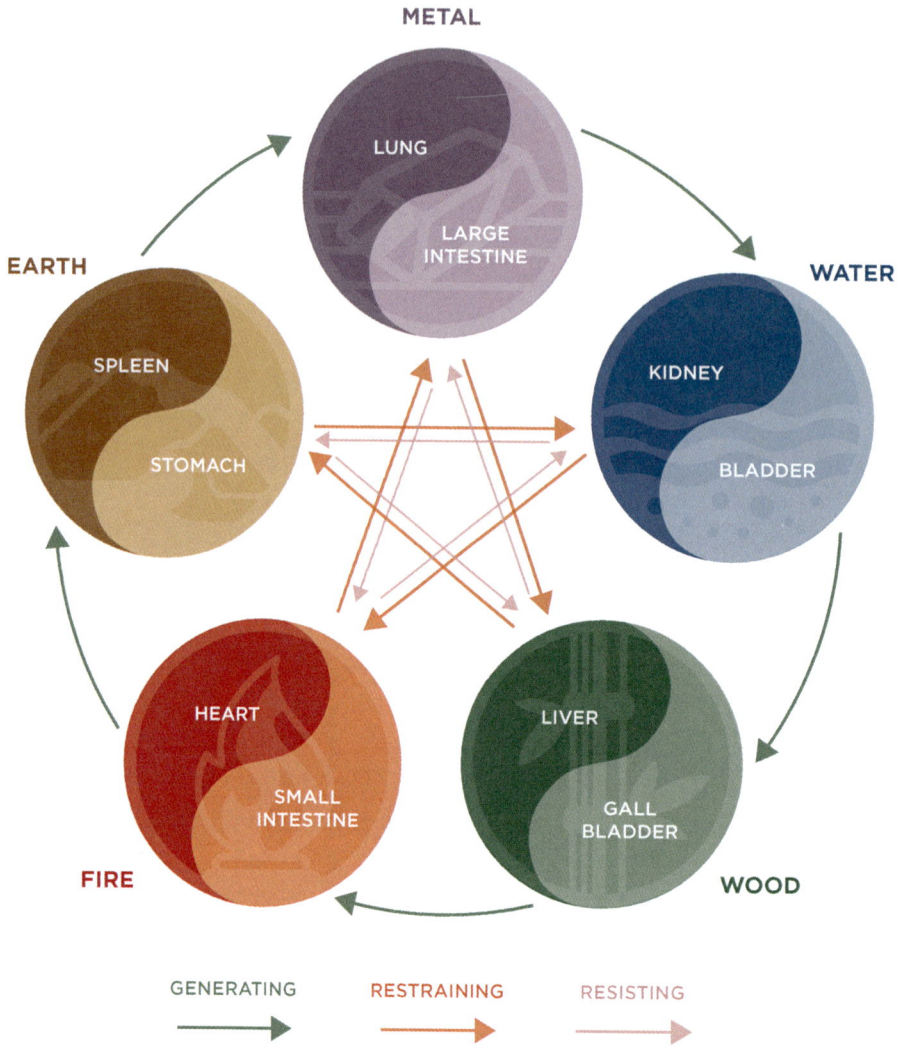

16   *Nourishing Wisdom for Life*

The Five Elements interact through three fundamental relationships in order to sustain balance: generating, restraining, and resisting. The generating cycle represents a relationship that generates, nurtures, and promotes growth. The restraining cycle represents a relationship that acts as an adversarial force that inhibits and disturbs the natural balance among the Five Elements. When an element overacts or exerts too much control over its subordinate element, it disrupts the harmonious balance and creates abnormalities. For example, the Earth element may soak up the Water element completely. The resisting cycle represents a reversal relationship that acts as a force to irritate and agitate the controlling element. This cycle occurs when the subordinate element acts defensively by returning the force imposed by the controlling element, again causing an imbalance. For example, instead of Earth suppressing Water, as in the Restraining cycle, Water would actually flood the Earth.

Examples of mutual generating:
- Metal promotes the quality of Water
- Water helps Wood grow
- Wood strengthens Fire
- Fire makes Earth (ash)
- Earth bears Metal

Examples of mutual restraining:
- Metal can cut Wood
- Wood can consume Earth
- Earth can contain Water
- Water can extinguish Fire
- Fire can melt Metal

Examples of mutual resisting:
- Metal can contain Fire
- Fire can temper water
- Water can flood Earth
- Earth can damage Wood
- Wood can erode Metal

TCM often only talks about the lung, spleen, heart, kidney, and liver—all *yin* or *Zang* organs—in diagnosis and treatments. This does not mean that their *yang*-paired organs are neglected; they are all related. Treating one organ always affects its paired organ. So, for example, treating the heart will always affect the small intestine. Each organ meridian corresponds to one of the Five Elements. However, since this section is a basic introduction of the law of the Five Elements, we will not discuss further how the meridians impact each other.

Emotions and the Five Elements

ELEMENT	*YIN* MERIDIAN	*YANG* MERIDIAN	EMOTION
Metal	Lung	Large Intestine	Grief
Earth	Spleen	Stomach	Sadness
Fire	Heart	Small Intestine	Joy
Water	Kidney	Bladder	Fear
Wood	Liver	Gall Bladder	Anger

As you may have noticed in the chart, emotion also plays a very important role in our health, and TCM monitors this connection carefully. I once asked Dr. Yang if the meridians had anything to do with people being unable to let go of a harmful memory of an unpleasant event in their lives. She said yes and explained that positive emotions pass through the meridians smoothly without leaving any toxin buildup, while negative events create negative *qi* which blocks the flow of the meridians. They stay in the body if not treated.

Grief affects the Lung and Large Intestine Meridians. TCM refers to immunity as defensive *qi*, and the Lung and Large Intestine Meridians host the defensive *qi* in the body. People's immune systems are weakened when they experience grief because *qi* flow is compromised in these meridians.

Sadness tends to slow down the spleen and the stomach in the digestive system.

We all agree that joy is a positive aspect of healthy living, but a prolonged period of joy may hurt one's body and can block the meridians of the heart and small intestine. Suppose a high school graduate is excited about being accepted into university, and as a result parties all summer long. He might not get enough sleep, and this may eventually lead to anxiety and reduced stamina. These symptoms are a sign of slower than normal *qi* flow in his heart and small intestine meridians.

Fear and worry hurt the Kidney and Urinary Bladder Meridians. Interestingly, in both Chinese and American cultures, there is a similar idiom about fear: "He was so scared he peed his pants." This expresses fear's negative impact on the kidneys and the bladder's physiological functions, which is also a sign for imbalanced *qi* in these meridians.

Anger obstructs the meridians of the liver and the gall bladder, like a car accident blocking highway traffic. Generally, anger affects one's appetite, which results in emotional eating, expressed as either binge eating or complete loss of appetite. Since both the liver and the gall bladder affect the digestive system, these two organs will end up functioning improperly as a result of excessive anger, and this will lead to a blockage of the corresponding meridians.

The Five Flavors of Food

In addition to their *yin* and *yang* properties, foods are classified by five flavors, each containing unique characteristics and imparting therapeutic effects: spicy, sweet, bitter, salty, and sour. If certain parts of the body or organs are weak or ill, eating the correct flavors of food that correspond to the five major organs will help to improve the condition.

FLAVOR	YIN ORGAN	YANG ORGAN
Spicy	Lung	Large Intestine
Sweet	Spleen	Stomach
Bitter	Heart	Small Intestine
Salty	Kidney	Bladder
Sour	Liver	Gall Bladder

- *Spicy or pungent foods* (*yang*) include ginger, green onion, chive, parsley, curry, chili, onion, black pepper, etc. They can expel wind and cold from the body. They help induce perspiration and invigorate energy circulation.
- *Sweet foods* (mostly *yang*) include honey, sugar, cherry, watermelon, carrot, banana, coconut, corn, milk, papaya, peanut, pumpkin, sweet rice, yam, lychee, longan, etc. Because some sweet foods are cool (*yin*) in property, they are used cautiously in postpartum food therapy when the new mother is already hyper-*yin*. Sweet foods can also help slow down acute symptoms, such as a fevers or colds, neutralize the toxic effects of other foods, and calm nerves.
- *Bitter foods* (*yin*) include radish leaf, bitter melon, olive, asparagus, lettuce, pickles, coffee, tea, dark chocolate, etc. They can clear heat or "fire," a Chinese term used for excessive heat build-up in the body.
- *Salty foods* (*yin*) include salt, kelp, seaweed, abalone, clams, cheese, etc. They can help the body to dissolve stagnation and re-balance electrolytes in the body.
- *Sour foods* (*yin*) include vinegar, grapefruits, lemon, lime, oranges, plums, tomato, berries, fermented vegetables, etc. They improve the functioning of the liver and gall bladder.

Besides exercising outdoors to replenish bodily *qi*, we often look for the right type of food to address health issues. For example, anger is usually included in, if not the cause of, elevated emotion. The liver meridian is affected by anger, and this results in the body producing heat, a phenomenon known as "fire" in TCM. A practitioner of Chinese medicine would advise sour food to extinguish the heat.

PART 2

THE ESSENTIAL MONTH

THE ESSENTIAL 30-DAY PERIOD OF REST AND STAYING IN AFTER BIRTH is the cornerstone of Chinese postpartum care.

Staying in for the Essential Month includes:

- Staying in the home
- Staying away from any air drafts or direct air vents
- Staying away from direct contact with cold water, which includes avoiding cold drinks
- Staying in bed (resting)

Now you can see why my mother was so busy after her grandchildren were born! Most household chores in this first postpartum month are done by mothers, mothers-in-law, or sometimes sisters. New mothers are restricted, for one month after giving birth, from doing any chores dealing with water and from going out in order to avoid exposure to wind or cold air.

The month immediately after giving birth is the most crucial time for a woman to restore her health and build the foundation of a healthy life. This is the time her body can absorb and benefit the most from the foods she eats and the health measures she takes. After the first Essential Month, the new mother's body does not absorb nutrients as readily as during this crucial postpartum period. Food is mixed with herbs to replenish the nutrients that the new mother gave her baby, and to restore the *qi*, the vital energy she lost in giving birth, especially a vaginal birth.

Rules for right after giving birth:

- Do not wash your hair until after at least a week, or up to one month.
  - It is recommended that the new mother waits at least one week to wash her hair, though not necessarily one month! Before there were hair dryers and central heating, the recommendation was a month since a new mother is exposed to cold air easily. Nowadays, hair dryers and indoor environments can help reduce this problem. However, be sure to dry off right after washing.
  - When a new mother does wash her hair for the first time after giving birth, she should put ginger peels saved from cooking into a big pot of water and boil them for 15–20 minutes. Then, she should use the ginger water to wash her hair. The ginger helps to expel *yin qi* and chills from the head.
- Do not go outdoors for at least one month.
- Do not walk with bare feet. Always wear house slippers or socks. There are a few pressure points at the bottom of each foot. One particular point is for the Kidney Meridian. The floor is generally cold and surrounded by *yin qi*, which travels up along this meridian. Too much *yin qi* will slow down recovery.

- Do not wear sleeveless or short sleeve blouses. Keep your arms warm.
- Do not take a full bath or shower for at least a week.
  - Similar to washing hair, do not shower the whole body the first few days after birth to avoid chill and damp air getting into the new mother's pores. However, washing the lower body is perfectly fine.
- Do not get into cold water.
- Do not drink cold drinks.
- Do not wash hands, dishes, or clothes with cold water.
- Do not eat raw vegetables or chilled food.
  - As stated above, the new mother's body has more *yin* than *yang qi* in her; cold beverages and cold food add more *yin* to the diet, which will not help the new mother to recover and gain strength as quickly. TCM and culture believe that if she does not regain her strength and restore her health during this crucial month, it will be very difficult for her to achieve this afterward.

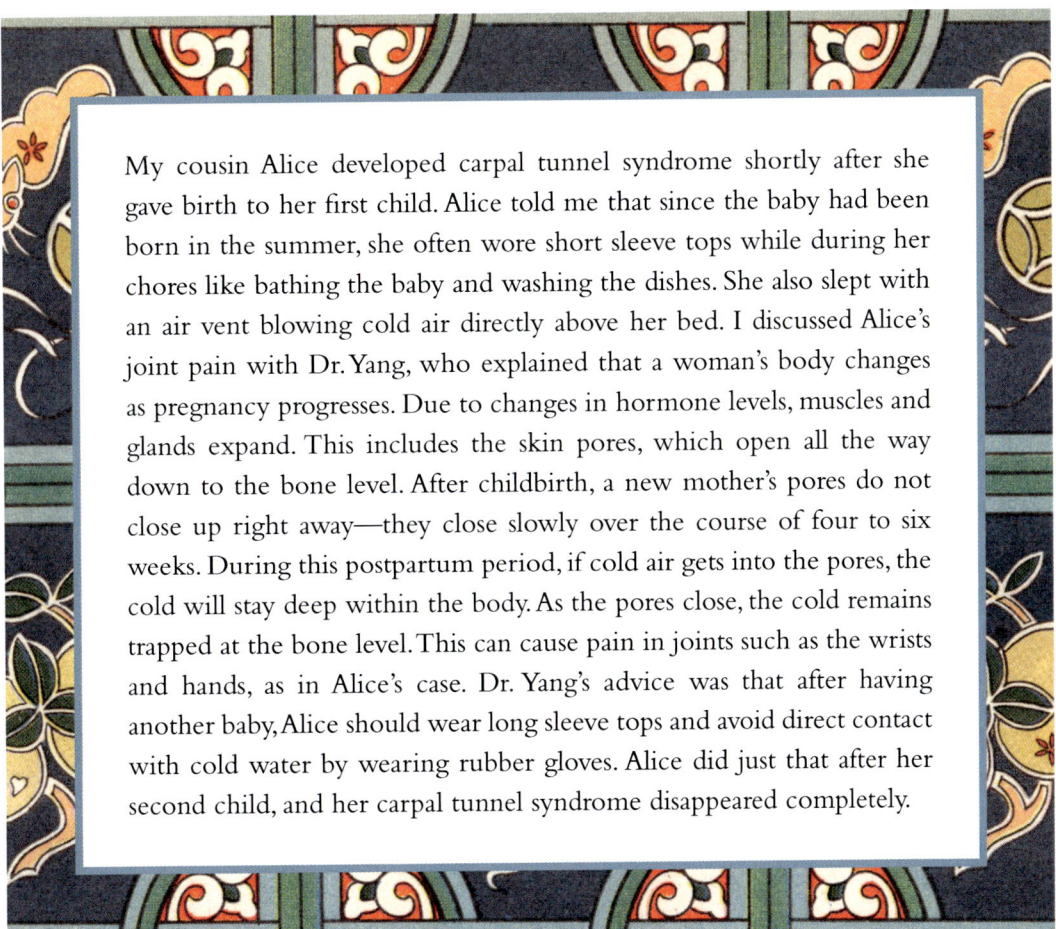

My cousin Alice developed carpal tunnel syndrome shortly after she gave birth to her first child. Alice told me that since the baby had been born in the summer, she often wore short sleeve tops while during her chores like bathing the baby and washing the dishes. She also slept with an air vent blowing cold air directly above her bed. I discussed Alice's joint pain with Dr. Yang, who explained that a woman's body changes as pregnancy progresses. Due to changes in hormone levels, muscles and glands expand. This includes the skin pores, which open all the way down to the bone level. After childbirth, a new mother's pores do not close up right away—they close slowly over the course of four to six weeks. During this postpartum period, if cold air gets into the pores, the cold will stay deep within the body. As the pores close, the cold remains trapped at the bone level. This can cause pain in joints such as the wrists and hands, as in Alice's case. Dr. Yang's advice was that after having another baby, Alice should wear long sleeve tops and avoid direct contact with cold water by wearing rubber gloves. Alice did just that after her second child, and her carpal tunnel syndrome disappeared completely.

RECIPES

TCM—as with most traditional medicine—sees very little difference between food and medicine. A good postpartum diet is essential to a new mother's full recovery. Therefore, I offer below many of the recipes I know, along with instructions on how to prepare and when to eat them. The recipes are mainly for soups and broths, which are easy to digest. They can be eaten as the main meal or as a side dish. Due to variances in location, cookware, size of available protein, etc., please make any desired adjustments to the ingredient proportions, cook times, and/or amount of water used. My recipe instructions are only meant to be a rough guide. Small changes in the consistency of the soup should not cause the food to lose its essential function. The key is to consume the essence of the broth or soup, which is derived from cooking the meat, bones, and/or herbs. It may seem overwhelming at first, but hopefully you can make them for your family and friends, and they may in turn make them for you!

The recipes are classified into three phases for the postpartum period:

- *Phase I*: This phase is dedicated to purging the toxins from any medication given during child birth and also in breaking down blood clots and purging other residues from the body. It allows the new mother to restore uterine function and help with the discharge of lochia (blood, mucus, and uterine tissue). While these recipes are classified as Phase I, they can be applied to Phase II as well. *A note on side dishes: during this phase, the new mother can consume fresh fruits and vegetables as long as they are at least at room temperature, though cooked vegetables are preferred during this period.*

- *Phase II*: This phase is dedicated to helping nourish the mother and replenishing her blood. It promotes metabolism and restores physical strength.

- *Phase III*: This phase is dedicated to restoring and strengthening the mother's *qi*, thereby allowing blood to circulate better and improve her overall physical condition.

These recipes are used as part of the new mother's daily diet (in addition to regular food) until one month after giving birth. While these are considered part of a special diet for new mothers, other people may eat them as well. Often relatives and friends are invited to enjoy this special food to help celebrate the birth of a child. Since it takes special effort to prepare this kind of food, and restaurants normally do not have this on their menus, one usually only finds them in a household where there is a newborn.

PHASE 1: PURGING, CLEANSING, AND STRENGTHENING

Ginger is incredibly important for purging and cleansing. It has been used for its health benefits for over 5000 years and is a favorite medicinal as well as culinary herb in Asian cuisine. Ginger is *yang* in nature; it produces warm effects to counter the *yin*. During birth, a great deal of cold and damp air is trapped inside the mother's body, which results in what we call gas. Gas is cold in nature; therefore, ginger is used generously in all the phases during the Essential Month, albeit in gradually-decreasing measures through the course of the month.

Ginger contains anti-viral, anti-toxic, and anti-fungal properties and is also used for the prevention of and treatment against cold symptoms. Due to its anti-inflammatory properties, it can be used to treat rheumatoid arthritis, osteoarthritis, and various other muscular disorders. Ginger contains special enzymes responsible for breaking down the proteins in the food, thus aiding in digestion and the prevention of cramps. Ginger has been proven to help lower cholesterol levels and prevent the formation of blood clots. This property makes it a natural decongestant as well as an antihistamine, making it the perfect remedy for colds. Not surprisingly, ginger contains Vitamin C, zinc, and magnesium.

Most of the teas, soups, and dishes prepared for new mothers in Phase I contain lots of ginger; in Phases II and III the amount slowly decreases. Ginger is also good for women during their menstrual periods to relieve cramps. It is also useful for people who catch a cold or after major surgeries.

One note: ginger is not for everyone. For those who have a heaty nature, too much ginger will drive more warm or hot *qi* into the body. Insomnia may occur, especially if consumed before bedtime in some people.

PHASE I: PURGING, CLEANSING, AND STRENGTHENING

TOASTED RICE AND GINGER TEA

This hot tea should be consumed immediately after child birth while the new mother is still in the hospital and during the first few days after child birth. She should consume this 2–3 times a day as part of her beverages. Most American hospitals serve iced tea, Jell-O, cold milk, or ice cream during the hospital stay, which is the exact opposite of what new mothers need. Whether the birth was vaginal or Caesarean, a new mother has exerted a tremendous amount of vital energy and has lost a lot of blood in giving birth. Expending this effort allows chill and damp air to enter into her body. This hot toasted rice and ginger tea will help in purging the air and gas out of a mother's body. Not only will it reduce gas pain, it will invigorate her. The ginger is yang in nature, thus it pushes the unwanted gas (chill) which is yin energy out of the body. The rice is a carbohydrate and will provide energy.

1 cup uncooked white rice

¾ cup thin julienne strips of ginger with peels on

Take approximately 1/5 lb. of fresh Ginger Root, and trim off any undesirable parts. Clean off the ginger with a damp paper towel but keep the peel on. (The peel is believed to have the most concentration of *yang qi*.) Cut the ginger into fine strips, as small as possible.

1. Use a clean dry wok or a large skillet.
2. Starting on low heat, pour unwashed rice into the wok, stirring thoroughly and frequently to avoid the rice turning brown too soon. Toast the rice until 75% of it turns golden to light brown. Remove from the wok. Discard any burnt rice.
3. Under low heat, toast the ginger strips, using the same process as the rice, stirring frequently. Always turn the ginger over from the bottom. It may take 20 minutes for the ginger to gradually dry and become medium brown. Raise the heat slightly if necessary. Toast the ginger until it is about 75% toasted, and it turns dry and brown. Pour the toasted rice in with the ginger and mix together. Continue to stir the mixture until the ginger loses almost all of its moisture and the rice turns golden brown.
4. Remove the mixture from the wok. Discard any severely burnt ginger. Allow the mixture to cool down on a plate. When cool, store in an air-tight container.
5. To make a cup of tea, bring 12-oz. of water to a boil in a sauce pan or kettle. An electric kettle will also work.
6. Add 2 teaspoons of the prepared tea mixture to the boiling water. Allow the tea to boil for 2–3 minutes. Reduce heat and simmer for another 2–3 minutes. Strain before drinking.

> **When and How Often Should a New Mother Drink This Tea?**
>
> A new mother should drink this tea after childbirth once her doctor says that she can drink clear broth or liquids. She should drink this as her primary beverage for the first few days after child birth, instead of plain water or iced tea.

PHASE I: PURGING, CLEANSING, AND STRENGTHENING

RED DATES, LONGAN, AND WOLFBERRIES TEA

After the new mother is discharged from the hospital, one of the warm beverages we prepare is a tea made with dried red dates, longan, and wolfberries. Red dates invigorate blood flow and help to nourish the liver and detoxify the body. It can increase the body's serum protein levels, which help to protect the liver and detoxify the body. It also helps to soothe the stomach. Longan fruit contains rich amounts of Vitamin C and minerals like iron, phosphorus, magnesium, and potassium. It is also rich in Vitamin A and essential in anti-oxidants, and it relaxes the nerves. Goji berries, or wolfberries, are known for improving eyesight, general well-being, strengthening the immune system, and providing cardiovascular protection. The portion below is good for one pot of tea which makes two cups.

15 goji berries or wolfberries 杞子
4 dried red dates (seedless) 紅棗
2 dried longan fruits 龍眼

1. Pre-measure the ingredients in a plastic sandwich bag. One bag per day will yield 2 cups.
2. Gently wash the ingredients once or twice before using. Boil 3 cups of water.
3. Add all the ingredients to the water. Bring to a boil and reduce to a simmer for 30 minutes or until reduced down to 2 cups of tea.

> **When and How Often Should a New Mother Drink This Tea?**
>
> A new mother should drink this tea for two weeks after childbirth.

PHASE I: PURGING, CLEANSING, AND STRENGTHENING

SUNG FAR TEA | 生化湯

Most Chinese herbal stores sell Sung Far *or* Sheng Hua *(the name in Mandarin) in a pre-measured package for two cups consumption. "Sung" promotes new blood. "Far" dissolves or reduces bruises.*

PRE-MEASURED PACKAGE

Angelica Sinensis, commonly known as *Dongquai* 當歸

Ligusticum Striatum or *Chuanxiong* 川芎

Chinese Licorice 甘草

Almond 桃仁

Dried Toasted Ginger

1. Use an enamel or clay pot and fill with 3 cups of water.
2. Empty the package of herbs in the pot. Bring it to a boil. Reduce heat to medium–medium high until the tea yields 1 cup.
3. Save the remaining herbs in the pot for a second repeated process.

> When and How Often Should a New Mother Drink This Tea?
>
> The new mother should take this tea 2–3 days after giving birth or after being discharged from the hospital. This tea stimulates blood growth and promotes healing of the uterine tissue or surgical wounds.
>
> Drink 1 cup once a day for 3–5 days.
>
> Note: The tea may be too strong or bitter for those who are not accustomed to drinking traditional Chinese herbal tea.

PHASE I: PURGING, CLEANSING, AND STRENGTHENING

MILK WITH GINGER

As previously mentioned, milk is encouraged for new mothers to consume, but as a hot drink. Cold milk is yin, and therefore milk should be boiled with ginger and consumed warm.

8 oz. of milk

2 thin slices of fresh ginger

Warm the milk on medium heat, add ginger and bring to a gentle, light boil for two minutes.

When and How Often Should a New Mother Drink This?

The new mother should drink this once discharged from the hospital as desired.

The ginger can be reduced to one slice after two weeks or when the new mother begins to feel dry in her tongue and lips, which are signs of *yang qi* being restored.

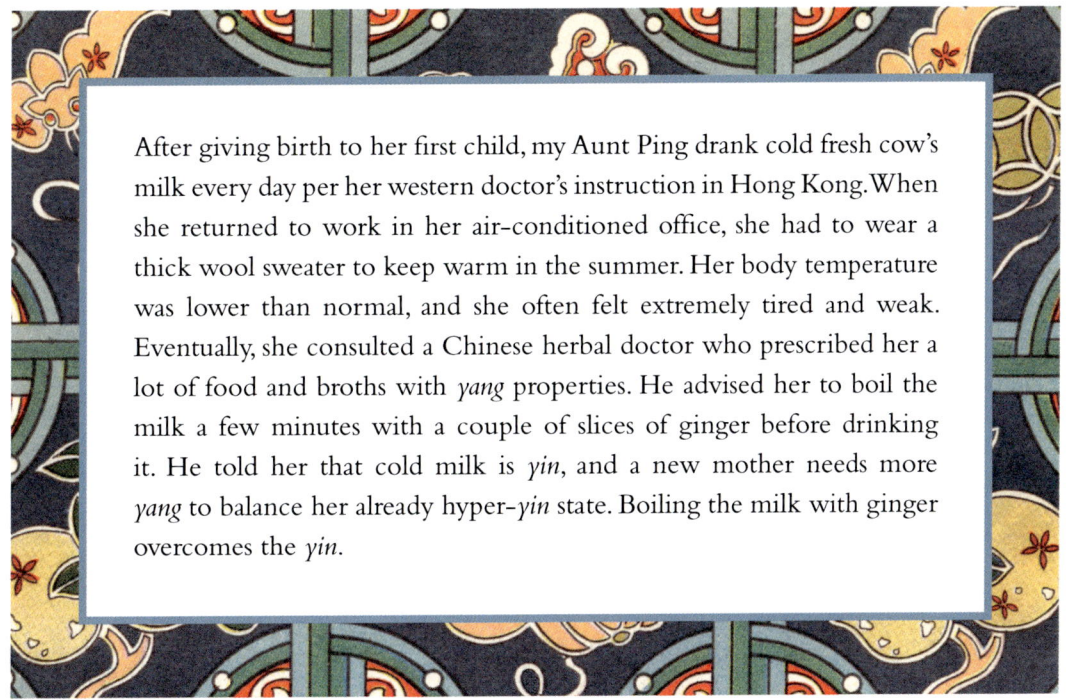

After giving birth to her first child, my Aunt Ping drank cold fresh cow's milk every day per her western doctor's instruction in Hong Kong. When she returned to work in her air-conditioned office, she had to wear a thick wool sweater to keep warm in the summer. Her body temperature was lower than normal, and she often felt extremely tired and weak. Eventually, she consulted a Chinese herbal doctor who prescribed her a lot of food and broths with *yang* properties. He advised her to boil the milk a few minutes with a couple of slices of ginger before drinking it. He told her that cold milk is *yin*, and a new mother needs more *yang* to balance her already hyper-*yin* state. Boiling the milk with ginger overcomes the *yin*.

PHASE I: PURGING, CLEANSING, AND STRENGTHENING

CHICKEN WINE SOUP

After a mother has given birth and is allowed to eat solid food, she should eat this home remedy. The alcohol (whether it's whiskey, brandy, gin, or rice wine, all of which are commonly used) helps with blood circulation and lactation. The majority of the alcohol will be cooked off with the heat. The black wood-ear fungus mushroom is known for its ability to nourish blood. This fungus is high in dietary fiber, iron, and Vitamins B1, B2, and C. It cleans blood vessels and the digestive system and reduces the risk of blood clots. Another ingredient in this remedy is dried lily flower bulbs. The dried lily flower bulb is known for its ability to moisten the lungs, soothe the upper respiratory system, clear away heat, and relieve liver stagnation, thus promoting restful sleep.

1½ lbs pork bones and lean pork for soup stock

1 whole chicken

½ cup sliced ginger root

2½ oz or 1 pkg black wood-ear fungus mushroom (sold in Asian markets or herbal stores)

1 pkg dried lily flower buds (sold in Asian markets or herbal stores)

¼ – ½ cup whiskey, gin, or brandy

½ Tbsp oil

5 quarts water

Add salt to taste

In preparation, clean the ginger by removing the peel, rinsing, and drying. Flatten ginger with the blade of a flat knife. Toast or brown the ginger in a heavy pan or wok on medium–medium high heat for a few minutes. Remove when it turns a light brown.

In separate large bowls, soak the black wood-ear mushrooms and lily flower buds for 1 hour. Thoroughly wash the black wood-ear fungus and remove any parts that are still hard. Cut into bite-size pieces. Also wash the lily flower buds thoroughly and rinse well. Remove any hardened ends. Scald the black wood-ear fungus and lily flower bud in boiling water. Remove after 30 seconds. Discard the water and set aside.

Prepare the pork bone stock by washing the bones first and parboil them with water in a large pot for 2 minutes. This helps to remove any excess fat. Discard the water, wash the bones, and set aside. Bring 5 quarts of water to a boil. Put the pork bones, meat, and chicken organs in and bring the soup back to a boil. Lower the heat to a simmer and slowly cook for 2 hours to make the stock. Skim off the grease, but continue to cook the soup on low heat. Clean the rest of the chicken, and cut into large pieces, bones and all. (I recommend having the butcher cut it up.)

1. Preheat a large size pot or a wok on medium heat. Add oil, and lightly brown the chicken pieces. Add ginger and mix quickly.

2. Pour half of the whiskey into the mixture. Simmer for a few minutes uncovered. Pour the chicken and ginger mixture into the pot with the bone stock. Cook for 30 minutes on low to medium heat or until chicken is 75% tender. Skim off the grease.

3. Add in the black wood-ear fungus and lily flower buds. Lower to medium heat and cook for another hour until the chicken is tender. Season to taste. Add the remaining whiskey before the heat is turned off. The black wood ear fungus can be eaten while it is still a bit crunchy. Consume while it is still warm.

4. Set aside the remaining soup. Once cooled down, it can be stored in soup containers and refrigerated or frozen. Before reheating, remove any grease that has congealed on top.

> **When and How Often Should a New Mother Eat This Soup?**
>
> The new mother should eat this several times a week after being discharged from the hospital until the pot of soup is finished. It can be eaten during meals or in between meals.

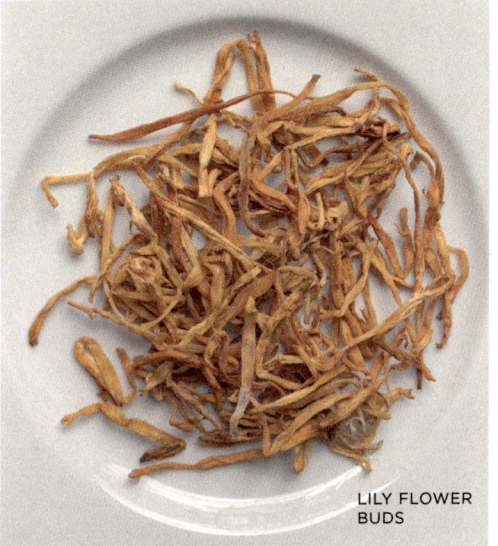

WOOD-EAR MUSHROOMS

LILY FLOWER BUDS

Phase I: Purging, Cleansing, and Strengthening

32 *Nourishing Wisdom for Life*

PHASE I: PURGING, CLEANSING, AND STRENGTHENING

PAPAYA, FISH, AND PEANUT SOUP

Southern Chinese believe that this soup helps the new mother with lactation. Both fish and peanuts are rich in protein. Papaya, which can be found in most supermarkets year round, is very rich in Vitamins A and C, folate, and potassium. Papaya contains papain, a digestive enzyme known for aiding in digestion as it cleanses the digestive tract, thus helping to prevent constipation. A study revealed that when consumed for a few days, it has a useful tonic effect in the stomach and intestines. The Chinese use papaya as a fruit and as a vegetable. New mothers are encouraged to eat this to help with lactation.

1½ lbs whole fish fillets (a white fish is recommended such as grouper, tilapia, or flounder)

1 whole ripe papaya (approx 8 inches long)

1½ cups shelled and peeled raw peanuts. Soak peanuts overnight. Drain before use.

4 large slices of ginger (If the new mother likes to eat ginger, prepare it in strips. If not, prepare it in slices so they can be easily discarded)

2 stalks green onion, cut into 1 inch pieces

2 tsp salt or add to taste

4 Tbsp cooking oil for browning the fish

4 cloves garlic (optional)

Salt and pepper to taste

2½ quarts of water

In preparation, cut the papaya in half. Remove the seeds with a large spoon. Cut each papaya half into 4 long slices. Remove the skin and cut into wedges.

Clean the fish fillets by removing scales (if any). Dry the fillets. Using a non-stick skillet on low heat, add 2 Tbsp of cooking oil. Once it is hot, add the ginger, a few pieces of green onion, and garlic. Quickly place half the fish fillets in the skillet. Gently sear and brown each side for 5 minutes. Repeat the process with the rest of the fillets. Do not fully cook the fillets. Cut each piece into half. Set aside.

1. Using a large soup pot, bring the water to a boil and add the ginger and peanuts. Cook on medium heat for 30 minutes or until peanuts are tender.

2. Add the fish fillets and papaya. Cover and cook over medium to high heat for 15 minutes. If you don't want the papaya to be cooked too soft, add the fish fillets first, let them cook down and add papaya at the end. Remember, papaya can be eaten uncooked. Skim off grease if needed. Taste and add seasoning as preferred.

> **When and How Often Should a New Mother Eat This Soup?**
>
> She can take this when she returns home from the hospital. Serve with a meal at least once per day. She could have this with her lunch and the Chicken Wine Soup with her supper!

PHASE I: PURGING, CLEANSING, AND STRENGTHENING

RICE WITH DRIED SCALLOPS AND BEEF

The Chinese use dried products from marine life generously as part of their diet for "boh", or replenishing. Dried abalone, dried scallops, dried oysters, dried seaweed, dried fish stomachs, etc., are all yin in property and therefore, these products serve to nourish the yin of the body. This recipe can all be made in a rice cooker.

1–2 whole dried scallops

8 oz. sliced flank steak

1 egg

¾ cup uncooked washed and rinsed white rice

1 tsp cut ginger strips

1 tsp olive oil

Water (and a measuring cup)

Dash of salt

1. Wash and soak the scallops in a small bowl of water for a few hours prior to cooking. Use your hands to separate or shred the scallop by hand; preserve the soaking liquid.
2. Put the shredded scallops into the rice cooker with the rice.
3. Pour the scallop water in a measuring cup and add tap water to make one cup liquid. Pour the liquid into the rice cooker.
4. Add the ginger strips, oil, and salt into the rice cooker. Press "cook" on the rice cooker.
5. In the meantime, slice pieces of the flank steak in the opposite direction of the grain for tenderness of the meat. Marinate steak with a pinch of salt, corn starch, and coat with olive or grapeseed oil. (This can be prepared in advance and keep them in separate bags in a freezer.)
6. On the rice cooker, when the cook button turns from "Cook" to "Stay Warm," crack the egg onto the rice. Stir and mix. (Optional: Also add pre-sliced flank steak at this step on top of the warm rice for a heartier meal.)
7. Cover for five minutes. Serve hot.

> **When and How Often Should a New Mother Eat This?**
>
> As part of the meal for the first two weeks and a few times during the third and fourth week. It depends on her appetite and willingness to eat.

PHASE II: NOURISHING

FISH HEAD SOUP

This soup is combined with two Chinese herbs: Chuanxiong (弓芎) and Angelica (白芷), which are known to expel chills from the head. As explained earlier, after giving birth, our pores—including those on our head—close slowly. Therefore, if a new mother exposes herself to a windy and chilly environment without wearing a head scarf or hat, cold, damp air will seep into her head and get trapped inside. Likewise, if she washes her hair too soon right after child birth and does not use a hair dryer right away, the cold damp moisture will be trapped in her scalp, which will result in long term chronic headaches. I have witnessed quite a few of my friends suffering from this. This remedy may not heal the chronic headaches due to improper care of the head after child birth, but it may at least help to reduce it. The herbs can be obtained from any Chinese herb store.

1 clean fish head (tip: brown the fish head with ginger before adding it to the soup in order to get rid of the fishy taste)

½ Tbsp of *Chuanxiong* 川芎

1 Tbsp of Angelica 白芷

1½ cups of boiling water

1 small piece of ginger

1. Put all the ingredients, along with 1½ cups of boiling water, in a heavy duty, oven-safe ceramic jar or pot with a lid.

2. Fill a stock pot with 4 inches of water. Place the ceramic jar in the stock pot. Cook for 2 hours over medium heat.

3. Add a dash of salt for taste.

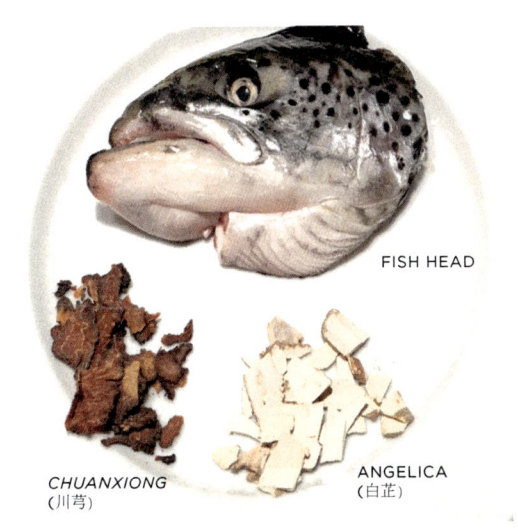

FISH HEAD

CHUANXIONG (川芎)

ANGELICA (白芷)

When and How Often Should a New Mother Eat This Soup?

A new mother should eat this anytime during her postpartum period. In addition, this soup is a general food remedy for people suffering from chronic headaches or migraines.

36 *Nourishing Wisdom for Life*

PHASE II: NOURISHING

PIGS' FEET, GINGER, AND SWEET DARK VINEGAR STEW

This stew has been consumed by new mothers in the Southern region of China for centuries. It is to be consumed twelve days after giving birth or when the mother finishes bleeding. The pigs' feet are rich in collagen, and their protein promotes healthy skin and strengthens muscle tone. They also provide a good source of calcium. The sweet-and-sour property not only stimulates the appetite but helps with cleansing. Vinegar dissolves the calcium from the bone of the pork knuckle to make it easier for absorption.

1 pair of pigs' "long feet", approximately 3-4 lbs total (1 front leg and 1 back leg, cut into small pieces by the butcher)

3-4 bottles of Chinese sweet black vinegar

½ lb ginger root

6-8 hard-boiled peeled eggs

½ cup white vinegar

In preparation, clean the pigs' feet. Boil water in a large pot and add the white vinegar to the water. Parboil the pigs' feet in the boiling water for two minutes. Remove the pigs' feet and set aside after two minutes.

Wipe the ginger clean with a damp paper towel and peel. "Smash" the bigger pieces with the blade of a cleaver. This will release the juices of the ginger into the soup. It will also allow the soup to be better absorbed into the ginger if you want to eat the ginger after cooking the soup. Brown the ginger in a skillet for a few minutes.

1. Pour the sweet black vinegar into a large ceramic pot or dutch oven (recommended).

2. Add the ginger. Bring the vinegar to a boil and add the pigs' feet. Bring the mixture to a boil, reduce heat and cook for 1 hour and 45 minutes, or until tender.

3. Test the pigs' feet for tenderness, extend cooking time as desired for pig's skin consistency.

4. Add the hard-boiled eggs into the mixture. Serve hot.

> When and How Often Should a New Mother Eat This?
>
> Once or twice a day after the twelfth day of the Essential Month. Around this time, she may feel dry in her throat, which means *yang* energy has been restored and the *qi* is in balance. She may begin to feel "warm" in her system. At this time, she should eat more vegetables and fruits which are cool in nature. Avoid cold foods, cold liquids, and too many raw foods.

Phase II: Nourishing

PHASE III: RESTORING

BLACK CHICKEN SOUP

Black chicken (also called Silkie Chicken) is sold frozen in Asian supermarkets. They are known for their lean meat with very little fat. The chicken flesh itself is dark gray or black, and the bones are black. They are free-range and slightly gamier in flavor. They are known for their superior nutrition to most chickens found at American supermarkets. However, the meat is tough and not the easiest to eat. But here we won't be roasting the chicken; the goal is to get a richer and more nourishing broth by combining the chicken with some traditional herbs. Many Chinese herbal stores pre-package the basic herbs for chicken soup.

PRE-MADE PACKAGE

Dongquai 當歸 (optional)

Chuanxiong 川芎 (optional)

Dried Angelica Root 白芷 (optional)

Dried Astragalus 北芪

Dried Codonopsis root 黨參

Red dates 紅棗

Wolfberries 杞子

Almonds (south) 南杏

Almonds (north) 北杏

American ginseng 花旗參

SOUP INGREDIENTS

1 whole black chicken

8 oz lean pork

A package of the Chinese herbs listed above. If purchased separately, use 2 pieces of each herb, 6–8 pieces of red dates, a tablespoon of wolfberries, a tablespoon of each type of the almonds, and 2 pieces of American ginseng

2–3 slices of ginger

Dash of salt

1. Defrost, wash, and rinse the black chicken.
2. Bring 2½–3 quarts of water to boil in a large stock pot. Add the chicken, lean pork, and ginger into the water and boil for 20 minutes.
3. Add the herbs into the pot. Bring to boil again, then reduce heat to low–medium heat for two hours.
4. Add a dash of salt to taste if needed.

Note: The herbs in this recipe have a bitter and strong taste. Those who are not accustomed to Chinese herbal soup may not appreciate it. However, these herbs can be substituted with a few pieces of American ginseng if desired.

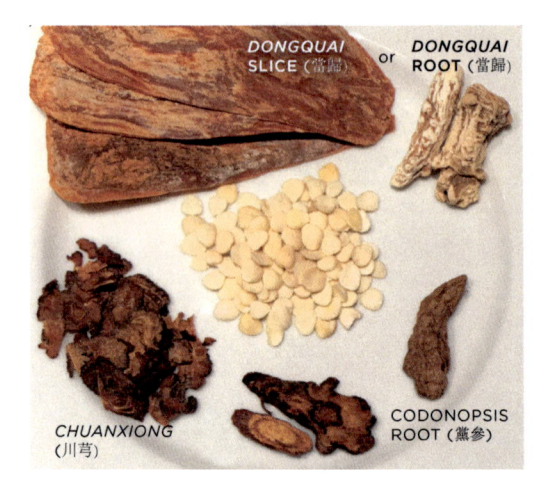

When and How Often Should a New Mother Eat This?

A new mother should eat this beginning the third week after child birth, a bowl each day for two days. Freeze the rest for the fourth week or thereafter.

Phase III: Restoring

PHASE III: RESTORING

GINSENG AND *DONGQUAI* TEA

Cold drinks such as iced tea, soda, and cold juice, are not recommended during the Essential Month, while the new mother is low in yang qi. *She should drink this tea instead. In the case of a new mother losing a lot of blood in child birth, this tea is highly recommended, as* Dongquai *is an essential herb to help build blood.*

2 thin slices of Korean ginseng
2 thin slices of *Dongquai* 當歸
4 cups of water

1. Put the ingredients into a pot of water, bring to a boil, and then lower the heat.
2. Continue to simmer for at least one hour and reduce to two cups.
3. Serve one cup while warm. Save the second cup in the refrigerator after it cools down.

> When and How Often Should a New Mother Drink This Tea?
>
> Consume two cups within a week or spread out to one cup per week for two weeks. If the tongue and throat feel dry, that means *yang qi* is restored. At this point the new mother should stop consuming this tea.

Note: There are mainly two types of ginseng: Asian or Korean ginseng and American ginseng. Ginseng is reported to have multiple benefits, boost energy, reduce stress, promote relaxation, strengthen the immune system, and enhance brain function. The Korean ginseng has more yang *properties than the American ginseng. The trunk of the ginseng is also more* yang *than the whiskers. It can cause insomnia as it acts as a stimulant in some people.*

SWEET STICKY RICE DESSERT

This dish is more traditional to the Mandarin than the Cantonese culture. Sticky rice (short grain glutinous rice) stimulates the intestines and strengthens digestive ability. However, over-consumption can lead to digestive problems as the stickiness of the rice requires the body to work a little harder to digest than as with regular long grain rice.

¼ cup short grain glutinous rice
3 cups water
2 Tbsp sugar
Seedless red dates (optional)

1. Bring water to a boil.
2. Add rice, red dates (optional) and sugar. Bring the mixture to a boil. Reduce heat and simmer for an hour.
3. Serve hot as a dessert.

> When and How Often Should a New Mother Eat This?
>
> The new mother should eat up to one bowl per day during the third or fourth week of postpartum.

PART 3

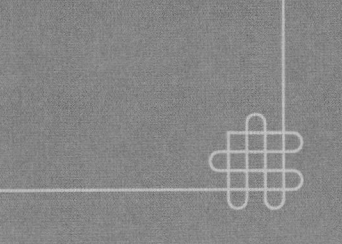

TCM TIPS FOR THE FAMILY

LET'S TALK ABOUT HOW TO APPLY THIS INFORMATION TO OUR DAILY LIVES, even if one has not just had a baby.

- Have you ever wondered why young people recover faster from a fall or an injury? It is because they have a tremendous amount of *yang qi* in them. *Yang* energy helps growth. It helps to build and repair cells. As we grow older, *yang* energy diminishes.

- How can we capture this *yang* energy? How do we harness it? If you stay indoors for prolonged periods of time, you will absorb a lot of *yin qi*. In order to harness *yang qi*, I would suggest that you spend some time each day outdoors and exercise for 20 to 30 minutes. Happily, this coincides with the recommendations of Western medicine.

  - The best time to get outside and exercise is in the morning, especially as the sun is rising, since it is the sun that brings forth an abundance of *yang qi*. Energy rises from the ground, propels the flowers to open up, and fills the atmosphere. If we stay outdoors, our body can absorb this fresh *yang qi* and thus help our cells to heal and rejuvenate faster. In the late afternoon, as the sun sets, *yang qi* slowly diminishes, and *yin qi* rises.

- Open the windows or doors 20–30 minutes on a sunny day every few days to allow *yang qi* to circulate into your house. The idea is to allow fresh *yang qi* into the house and help push the stagnant *yin qi* out. Open the blinds and allow sunlight to come through the house during the day. Again, this advice is not actually all that surprising, whether or not one has heard of *qi*.

- After exercise, especially when exertion is heavy, when the body is hot and sweaty, allow 30 minutes or so to cool down before consuming icy cold drinks. Drink room temperature or even warm liquids to allow the body to continue to perspire and purge toxins. Hot lemon and honey water is highly recommended after a lot of sweating. Icy cold drinks will tend to shock the body and deter the purging of toxins.

- In the summer before going outdoors to exercise, raise the thermostat. That way, after you exercise you will not return to a frigid house until you have allowed your body to naturally cool down or dry off. This will prevent the cold air from going into the skin pores while they are opened for perspiration.

- Do not sit too long if you can help it. Get up every hour or so for a few minutes to loosen up or move around. This will help to strengthen the kidney meridians. The urinary bladder meridians are located along our back; they run from the head to the hips and down to the feet behind the legs. If one sits too long, these meridians are suppressed, the bladder weakens, and the body retains excess water.

GINGER AND RED SUGAR TEA

The principles of yin *and* yang *can also help women who are not pregnant. Many women suffer from PMS, and for some, cramps can be very painful, even debilitating. This tea has stopped the monthly miseries of many of my daughters' young college friends. Though it seems a simple remedy, there is a theory behind it.*

During menses, a woman's body is in the yin *cycle, therefore, her body temperature drops a bit during the first few days of menstruation. Ginger, being* yang *in nature, helps to push the dead blood out from the uterus while the red sugar, which is also* yang *in nature, helps boost energy and blood circulation. According to TCM, cramps are a result of dead blood clots in the uterus. This tea aids the body in expelling these clots.*

3-4 slices of fresh ginger

1-2 tsp of red sugar (red sugar is a processed product from regular cane sugar. White cane sugar is *yin*, but red sugar and black sugar are *yang*). Red sugar can be obtained at Chinese supermarkets. Brown sugar will also suffice.

1. Boil the ginger root in one cup of water for 15–20 minutes and add 1–2 teaspoons of red sugar.

2. On the first and second days of your cycle, consume the tea while it is still hot.

3. From the third day thereafter, wait for the tea to cool and then drink it.

After drinking the tea, the bleeding may look heavier—this is a good sign. The old, dead blood is being purged. With regular drinking of the tea, blood flow should return back to normal after a few months, and eventually the uterus is cleaner and cramps are reduced. As is the case with the Essential Month, cold drinks and food are not recommended during menstruation since they will slow down the flow of blood. Similarly, during the week of her period, a woman should not wash her hair and leave it to air dry, as the cold air will seep into the pores of the head and cause headaches.

STORIES

Before I end this book, I'd like to include some personal stories, both to try and explain how the principles of *yin* and *yang qi* work a bit more concretely, and to show you, dear reader, how I gained this knowledge. I paid attention to the many lessons I learned and the situations around me.

My Friends

I have had the occasion to visit friends in the hospital who have just had hysterectomies, each of whom was suffering because of the food and drink given to her in the hospital. First, each was given water with ice to drink, and then each was told she could not eat solid food until she passed gas, so she was given Jell-O to eat. All of them felt very bloated and miserable. I made Roasted Ginger & Rice teabags for them to make hot tea in their rooms. Shortly after consuming the tea, each of my friends was able to pass gas and were very relieved as she could begin to eat solids. The principles of the Essential Month also apply to my friends: during their surgeries, air got into their stomach—this air is *yin* in nature. Then each of my friends was given cold food, which is also *yin*. Though it is possible to heal with food and drink without *yang* properties, a *yang* beverage helps expedite the process. The tea did the job.

The Nile River Cruise

My husband and I took a cruise along the Nile River many years ago. One of the stops was touring the pyramids in the Sahara Desert. The outdoor temperature was about 118°F. We set out after lunch and returned to the ship a few hours later. The passengers were told not to go directly to our cabins when we returned, but instead were to stay on deck for some warm lemon and honey water. They encouraged everyone to stay outside for 20 minutes. Everyone followed this advice except for two American couples. They refused the warm lemon and honey water and instead went straight to the bar to drink cold beer and sodas.

This same night on the cruise was the Captain's Dinner. While we were having dinner, we heard a siren from an ambulance approaching our ship, and a few medical personnel boarded. We were informed by the wait staff that four Americans had gotten sick. It was confirmed that they were the two couples who went straight to the bar a few hours beforehand. They claimed they had food poisoning, as they all had high fevers and were vomiting. The problem with this diagnosis, however, was that we had all eaten the exact same food. Additionally, the beer and soda they drank were sealed bottles from America. The ship's crew explained that these four people got sick because they did not cool down on deck and refused the warm lemon and honey water. The crew continued reporting that the extremely hot temperature of the desert and the cold temperature of our cabins and the interior of the ship would shock our bodies. The cooling off at the deck allowed our bodies to adjust.

When I came back home, I told Dr. Yang this story. She went further, explaining that the extreme heat had made us perspire, and that perspiration is a form of purging for the body. At the peak of this purging, toxins are excreted into the stomach, and they move from the stomach to the colon for excretion. The citrus of the lemon helps the process of excretion, and warm drinks expedite the process as well. Therefore, the American couples stopped the purging process by not allowing their bodies to cool down, and cold air from the air conditioning went straight to their open pores. Plus, the cold beer and cold soda stopped any toxins from leaving the stomach, creating food poisoning-like symptoms.

The Cook

When I was a college student in Miami, I worked as a waitress in a Chinese restaurant on the weekends. The owner, Mr. Chow, was also the chef. One day, he was very sad as he heard that another good friend of his died suddenly of a heart attack. His friend was also a cook; Mr. Chow had heard that his friend drank several beers right after he cooked when he took his break and collapsed. Strangely, this was not the first time he knew of a cook who had collapsed in the same manner and under the same circumstances. Mr. Chow told me that the kitchen of a Chinese restaurant is always very hot due to the flames of the woks. The cooks were directly affected as they stood in front of the stoves for hours. Even though they felt hot, they should not drown themselves with cold beer as soon as they finished cooking because the sudden temperature difference could kill them. He showed me an article from a New York Chinese newspaper addressing this issue and warning Chinese cooks.

The Teenager

One time when translating for Dr. Yang, I encountered a 16-year-old boy who was accompanied by his mother. This young man wanted to go to summer camp that year, but his doctor advised against it, due to the fact that the boy had an irregular heartbeat. In fact, the doctor and the boy's father both wanted to insert a pacemaker in order to remedy his irregular heartbeat. The boy's mother, however, was skeptical, and so she took her son to consult with Dr. Yang.

In taking the boy's history, he revealed that right after football practice at school, which occurred several times a week, he drank ice-cold drinks. Dr. Yang went on to explain that while some people can handle extremely cold beverages right after heavy exercise, others cannot. The boy's body seemed not to be able to handle the shock. The icy cold drink went to his stomach, shocked his small intestines, then affected his lungs, which in turn affected his heart. Dr. Yang worked on his heart and liver meridians for a few sessions, and asked him to avoid cold drinks right after football practice. He went back to his cardiologist for another test. His heartbeat was no longer irregular and he was given the green light to go to camp when school let out that summer.

CONCLUSION

Whether one calls it the Postpartum Month, the Essential Month, or the Staying in Month, it all means the same: the first month after giving birth is the most crucial month to give a new mother a chance not only to regain her health and strength, but also to correct whatever unhealthy symptoms she may have had before the birth of her child. It is my sincere hope that readers both Chinese and not will benefit from some of this information passed down by generations of Chinese women and healers.

ACKNOWLEDGMENTS

IVY YANG is the daughter of Dr. Yong Shu Yang. She has worked closely with me in providing guidance and advice on the technical aspects of this book. She is an expert in YSY Medicine, Holistic Integrative Medicine, Energy Medicine, and Mind Body Spirit. Ivy is a graduate of Columbia University with a Master Degree in Public Health. She is also a writer, an educator, and an entrepreneur.

KATHERINE QUAN AHMANN, my youngest daughter, is a brilliant graphic designer who laid out this book from cover to cover. Without her dedication, talent, and creativity, this book would not have its intuitive illustrations and diagrams that serve to demonstrate many of the complex principles.

DR. CAROLINE QUAN LONG and **KRISTEN QUAN HAMMILL** are my other two daughters who helped inspire me to write this book. Without their encouragement, I may not have shared these recipes and concepts for their children and future generations.

BIBLIOGRAPHY

Lu, Henry C. *Chinese System of Food Cures*. New York: Sterling Publishing Co., Inc., 1986.

Yang, Yong Shu. *YSY Medicine*, vol. I and II (Chinese). Zhuhai, China: Zhuhai Publishing House, 1997.

Yang's Natural Healing Center. *Yong Shu Yang Therapy* (Chinese). Zhuhai, China: Meridian Activation and Relaxation Research Center, 1992.

ABOUT THE AUTHOR

Sylvia L. Quan was born in the Seychelles and grew up in mainland China and Hong Kong before coming to the United States to attend college. She settled in Texas, earning a bachelor's degree from the University of Houston. Sylvia subsequently taught Chinese language and culture to elementary school students before helping her husband, Gordon, start his immigration law firm in Houston. She continues to manage his law practice to this day. Together, they have three daughters and five grandchildren.

Sylvia developed an interest in Chinese medicine while living in Hong Kong. After arriving in Houston, she developed several chronic medical conditions that Western medicine could not treat. The situation led her back to traditional Chinese remedies for healing, such as acupuncture, herbal medicine, and energy healing. At her daughters' urging, she has spent the past several years developing this book to provide insights into and illustrate the fundamental principles of traditional Chinese medicine and energy therapy. Sylvia wishes to highlight these practices' unique cultural approach to health in terms of food and environment. She hopes others may benefit from her sharing her knowledge and unique experiences.

Made in the USA
Middletown, DE
26 August 2022